752

Stanley Spencer

Stanley Spencer

VISIONS FROM A BERKSHIRE VILLAGE

Duncan Robinson

Phaidon · Oxford

Phaidon Press Limited, Littlegate House, St Ebbe's Street, Oxford

First published 1979
Published in the United States of America
by E. P. Dutton, New York
© 1979 Phaidon Press Ltd
All rights reserved

ISBN 0 7148 1970 0
Library of Congress Catalog Card Number: 78-73501

Printed in Great Britain by Waterlow (Dunstable) Ltd

1 (frontispiece). *Self-portrait, 1913*. Oil on canvas, 60.3 × 50.8 cm. (23¾ × 20 in.) London, Tate Gallery

List of Plates

Select Bibliography

R. H. W [Wilenski], *Stanley Spencer*, Ernest Benn, London, 1924.

Elizabeth Rothenstein, *Stanley Spencer*, Phaidon Press, Oxford and London, 1945.

Eric Newton, *Stanley Spencer*, The Penguin Modern Painters, Harmondsworth, 1947.

R. H. Wilenski, *Stanley Spencer: Resurrection Pictures 1945–50*, with notes by the artist, Faber & Faber, London, 1951.

John Rothenstein, *Modern English Painters*, *Lewis to Moore*, Eyre & Son, London, 1956.

Gilbert Spencer, *Stanley Spencer*, Gollancz, London, 1961.

Maurice Collis, *Stanley Spencer*, Harvill Press, London, 1962.

Elizabeth Rothenstein, *Stanley Spencer*, Express Art Books, London, 1962.

Colin Hayes, *Scrapbook Drawings of Stanley Spencer*, Lion and Unicorn Press, London, 1964.

Louise Collis, *A Private View of Stanley Spencer*, Heinemann, London, 1972.

Carolyn Leder, *Stanley Spencer, The Astor Collection*, Thomas Gibson Publishing Ltd, London, 1976.

Duncan Robinson, ed., with contributions from Richard Carline, Carolyn Leder, Anthony Gormley, Robin Johnson. *Stanley Spencer*, exhibition catalogue, The Arts Council of Great Britain, 1976.

Richard Carline, *Stanley Spencer at War*, Faber & Faber, London, 1978.

Introduction

'Don't try to make a boiled-down, simplified version of anything I say . . . the second-hand examples I have seen of myself I could not recognize.' His own words are a salutary warning to anyone who tries to write about Stanley Spencer. Yet the challenge is an inviting one. Twenty years after his death his paintings continue to command both interest and attention. More so perhaps than any other twentieth-century English painter, he has sustained a level of popularity reached in his case right at the end of his career when his native village of Cookham finally awoke to its own immortality bestowed by the efforts of his brush. Characteristically, Spencer found more than a little wry pleasure in the situation. He responded to fame simply but effectively, explaining his imaginative paintings and the ambitious schemes into which they fitted with the same simple directness he possessed as a child. When his younger brother Gilbert had asked him what angels were, he had replied: 'Great white birds what pecks.' Fifty years later, writing in the same spirit, he explained of *The Resurrection with the Raising of Jairus's Daughter*, 1947 (fig. 60), 'in order to further make clear my feelings of happiness, I put over the door the usual "Welcome Home" signs and flags and bunting they put up for soldiers returning from the war'. Needless to say, the homecoming in all his cosy, late Apocalypses

is to Cookham, which remained for Spencer the 'holy suburb of heaven', where angels shared the pavements with Fred Duckett and walls and high fences separated the passers-by from events like the Nativity and John Donne arriving in heaven. His younger brother recalled their view of the world from the nursery: 'Stan and I could well imagine that the Shepherds watching their flocks would have been in the field below Cliveden Woods. That was the land of the Nativity for us.' Stanley Spencer never lost that faith in the local presence of the supernatural, just around the corner or over the hedge.

Nevertheless, he did look back to his earlier work, before the First World War, with a strong nostalgia. 'Those pictures have something I have lost,' he told Sir John Rothenstein. By so saying he encouraged his critics to concentrate their praise upon the first decade of his activity. He was able to do so partly because he enjoyed recognition at a relatively early stage in his career. He attracted the attention of his most important patrons within a very few years of leaving the Slade as a prize pupil. In 1924, three years before his first major retrospective exhibition at the Goupil Gallery, Ernest Benn published the monograph on him by R.H.W(ilenski). To count, in addition, Sir John and Lady Rothenstein among his champions in print before he reached the age of forty was no mean achievement. And if their preference for the early works followed

7

Spencer's own, it is both a compliment to his judgement and a measure of their respect for it. However, the effect has been to obscure the extraordinary continuity of vision which runs throughout his working life.

For Spencer was endowed with a prodigious visual memory which enabled him to recall and represent details long after he had first observed them. He was also a prolific draughtsman who could revive working drawings to serve as models for paintings years after their original execution. *The Farm Gate* (fig. 65), for instance, painted as his Diploma Picture for the Royal Academy in 1950, shows the entrance to the farmyard as it must have been seen by Spencer in his youth, looking down from one of the bedroom windows of Fernlea, his home in Cookham High Street. A detailed preparatory drawing for the painting, squared for transfer, survives, dated 'June 16th, 46'. Certain subjects also recur to give a thematic unity to his life's work. Above all, there is the Resurrection, represented first in 1915, a *point de repère* in 1926 (fig. 20), the focal point of the Burghclere Chapel in 1932 (fig. 26) and the culmination of his wartime experiences in Port Glasgow, 1940–5 (fig. 59). Similarly his devotion to his first wife Hilda survived the disaster of their marriage to emerge in the undisguised nostalgia of paintings such as *Love Letters* of 1950 (fig. 63). Her death in the same year interrupted neither the adulatory paintings nor his one-sided correspondence with her. The love letters quite literally continued. Spencer completed *Love on the Moor* in 1954 (fig. 67) and left unfinished at the time of his own death five years later his final tribute, extended over more than 120 square feet, the *Apotheosis of Hilda*.

It is hardly surprising, given the importance and unusual nature of the subject-matter in so many of Spencer's paintings, that his critics have tended to concentrate upon their content at the expense of their form. Once again,

Spencer encouraged that approach, by the impatience he occasionally showed towards the end of his life with the actual process of painting: 'It does not whet my appetite to paint at all,' he confided in a letter of 1957 written to Hilda, after her death. As a result, there has been a tendency to rely upon a literary interpretation of his work. 'With him', Eric Newton wrote in 1947, 'each picture is a statement of a particular message, an illustration of a specific idea in pictorial form.' This view of Spencer, as the exponent of a personal philosophy who just happened to paint, ignores a considerable section of his output. Although he was inclined to denigrate his skill as a landscape painter, because of his dependence upon it for a steady income, it was considerable. What is more, Spencer's sensitive handling of natural detail plays an important part in many of the large-scale compositions, where the freshness of observation—the play of sunlight upon a particularly lush stretch of water-meadow, for instance —reveals both his skill as a painter and his unfailing response to the medium.

Spencer could be equally dismissive of his portraits, but if economic pressure occasionally persuaded him to undertake an otherwise unrewarding commission, that was not true of the series of self-portraits which punctuate his career at regular intervals from 1913 to 1959. The deep shadows of the softly modelled face in the portrait of 1913 (fig. 1) are replaced in 1936 (fig. 41) by bright light, informing the much harder, gleaming flesh and the radiant confidence of the features. In turn that gives way to tight-lipped defiance in the *Self-portrait* (fig. 70) painted only months before the artist's death in 1959. In this last, the dry paint, thinly applied, conveys the reality of desiccated flesh out of which the two irregular eyes stare, in contrast, with liquid determination. Only a painter with a deep-seated instinct for paint as a means of expression could have achieved within the medium such daunting feats of self-analysis.

In the years following Spencer's death, the inevitable biographies appeared. First in the field was his brother, Gilbert Spencer, whose book, published in 1961, recalled their childhood together, their early training as artists and their subsequent contacts. Its frankly personal approach is its strength and its value, offering as it does incomparable insights into the formative years they shared, as brothers and artists. Recently it has been joined by Richard Carline's *Stanley Spencer at War* (1978). This also deals with the earlier part of Spencer's career, recounted largely in Spencer's own words, from hitherto unpublished letters and writings in the author's possession. Where possible, Carline's corrected dating of early works has been followed in this account. Spencer's former brother-in-law makes a sympathetic editor who adds insights from his own contact with his subject in the large circle of artists they both knew and shared as friends. Apart from these personal accounts, there is the official biography which was commissioned by Spencer's executors from Maurice Collis and published in 1962. It is based upon Spencer's own writings, the vast collection of unsorted papers made available to the author as the source material for his book. He found in them what amounted to an unwritten autobiography from which he constructed his own version of the artist's life, to which the paintings serve merely as biographical illustrations. *A Private View* by Louise Collis, which was published in 1972, is concerned solely with the *dramatis personae* of the life and with certain adjustments to their roles. It provides a less charitable account of Spencer's actions and offers no new insights into his artistic activity.

Fortunately, however, an artist's reputation rests, in the long run, upon his art. This book contains a large number of illustrations which to a great extent speak for themselves. My commentary relies, inevitably, upon Spencer's own writings and upon the biographies which explain the meaning of his pictures by relating them to the events of his life. I have tried to redress the balance, however, against the generally accepted view of Spencer as a solitary artistic phenomenon. Like all artists, he had affinities with the art of his present as well as with that of the past. His individual talent developed in the context of particular artistic traditions, which he shared with his contemporaries, in one of the most vital and productive periods of English art. It was within that context that he was able, as a painter, to make real his vision, to embody in paint what were for him the eternal truths of his earthly paradise on the River Thames.

Cookham

Stanley Spencer was born in the Berkshire village of Cookham on 30 June 1891. This simple fact enjoys, in his case, a more than usual significance, for he was to identify throughout his life, to an extraordinary degree, with his birthplace and its immediate Thameside hinterland. The eighth surviving child of William and Anna Spencer, he grew up in the relative security of a somewhat impoverished, late Victorian household. His father, 'Professor of Music, Organist of St. Nicholas, Hedsor' according to the brass plate outside Fernlea, the family house in the High Street, made a modest but adequate living as a teacher of music. The regular procession of pupils combined with the performing members of the Spencer household to provide for the upbringing of the younger children a constant accompaniment. Spencer's brother Gilbert, his junior by thirteen months, recalled that from an early age 'listening to the music was no longer a conscious process; it had become as much a part of our lives as breathing'.

Life in the nursery was enclosed: 'There were hidden bits of Cookham as remote as the Milky Way'—Gilbert Spencer once more. Both brothers retained the most intensely vivid impressions of childhood. Stanley Spencer's painting of *Christmas Stockings*, 1936, is based upon one of his drawings for the month of December, made in 1926 for the Chatto and Windus *Almanack* of the following year. The foreground of the painting is extended to include a memory of Fernlea described by Spencer in a broadcast of 1955: 'in the nursery the cracks in the floorboards were rather wide. . . . I cut nuns out of cardboard and set them walking in procession.' The Spencer children were not sent out to school. Their father had fixed ideas on that as well as other educational topics, and to cater for them as well as to supplement his income, he set up a small school of his own in a shed at the bottom of the garden next door. By the time Stanley and Gilbert Spencer were old enough to benefit, the teaching had been entrusted to their two older sisters, Annie and Florence. As a result, neither of the boys acquired anything resembling a formal education. Instead they were given the freedom to pursue their own interests, in Stanley's case, drawing and reading, with a marked preference for his father's kind of texts. Mr Spencer was in the habit of reading aloud to his family, from the Bible chiefly, and of reciting poetry. This, together with regular attendance at both church and chapel, and doses of Bible reading prescribed for them by their mother, gave the Spencer children an early and uncritical familiarity with the stories of the Old and New Testaments. Cookham and the Bible—these were the two ingredients in Spencer's childhood, inextricably bonded into the unshakable foundations of his subsequent outlook on life.

Stanley Spencer's interest in art, shared by his younger brother, was new in a family of predominantly musical talents. In the course of their walks on Cookham Moor and Odney Common, the boys got to know William Bailey, a local amateur artist, whose daughter, Dorothy, gave them their first lessons in painting. In 1907, when Spencer was sixteen, his father agreed that he should go as an art student to the Technical Institute in nearby Maidenhead. There he received his first taste of formal training, recalled, years later, in one of his scrapbook drawings of a class copying from the antique (fig. 2). In style, the drawing belongs to a much later phase of his career. His early work betrays a heavy dependence upon the nineteenth century, especially upon the drawing of the Pre-Raphaelites. *The Fairy on the Waterlily Leaf* (fig. 4), drawn three years after his spell at Maidenhead, reveals the young artist's affection for the crisp, clear outline and precise detail characteristic of so much English book illustration from Rossetti and Millais (fig. 3) to Arthur Rackham and Walter Crane. Indeed, Gilbert Spencer recalled that while still in the nursery his brother was heard to express a wish to draw like Arthur Rackham.

After a year at Maidenhead, Spencer applied successfully to the Slade School. He was encouraged to do so by Lady Boston, the wife of his father's chief patron, who spotted his talent and offered to pay the fees there. She did so until 1910, when Spencer won a scholarship to cover them. There he joined the distinguished group of future artists who were his contemporaries as pupils of Henry Tonks, one of the most enlightened teachers of his day and a fervent champion of sound draughtsmanship. Spencer was just one of a generation of students at the Slade whose subsequent work remained faithful to those passionately implanted precepts.

His fellow students included David Bomberg, Mark Gertler, Paul Nash, C. R. W. Nevinson

2. *Gladiator at the
Technical School,
Maidenhead.* About
1939–40. Pencil on paper,
40.6 × 27.9 cm. (16 ×
11 in.) Astor Collection
of Scrapbook Drawings.
Inscribed verso:
'A memory of my days
at the Technicle [sic]
School. Two students are
talking to each other by
their drawing boards.
The local governors
(mayor and councillors)
are on an official visit.
The figure is the
Gladiator. Casts are on
the shelves and hanging
on the wall. And like the
comic post card I saw of
two tramps saying to
each other about a cow in
a field. Just think everywhere it looks it sees
something to eat, so here
everywhere one looked
there was something to
draw or being drawn.
On the left is the back
of the head of an old lady
doing a water colour of
rock gooseberry which
was always being
done . . .'

3. Sir John Everett Millais (1829–1896): *Claudio and Isabella*. 1848.
Pen and ink, 22.5 × 31.4 cm. (8⅞ × 12⅜ in.) Cambridge, Fitzwilliam Museum

and Edward Wadsworth. To them he was known as 'Cookham', because he continued to live at home, travelling up by train to Paddington each day to attend classes. Even so, he made friends. *John Donne Arriving in Heaven* (fig. 5) was bought by one of them, Jacques Raverat. Raverat and his future wife, Gwen Darwin, had given Spencer a copy of Donne's *Sermons*, from which the inspiration for the picture was drawn. Gilbert Spencer explained it further: 'He had the idea that heaven was to one side: walking along the road he turned his head and looked into Heaven, in this case a part of Widbrook Common.' Another gift from the Raverats at

about the same time was a copy of John Ruskin's study of *Giotto and his Works at Padua*. Like Donne, Ruskin was familiar to Spencer from his father's repertory, and at this stage in his development, Ruskin had an especial appeal. 'Giotto was to his contemporaries', Spencer read, 'precisely what Millais is to *his* contemporaries. A daring naturalist, in defiance of tradition, idealism, and formalism.' Thus the young devotee of the Pre-Raphaelites began to look back towards some of their heroes and, to judge from *John Donne* alone,

4. *The Fairy on the Waterlily Leaf.* 1910. Pen and ink, 41.9 × 30.5 cm. (16½ × 12 in.) Cookham, Stanley Spencer Gallery

5. *John Donne Arriving in Heaven.* 1911. Oil on canvas, 36.8 × 40.6 cm. (14½ × 16 in.) Private Collection

his knowledge of them was second-hand. 'In the first place, Giotto never finished highly,' Ruskin wrote. 'Even in his smallest tempera pictures the touch is bold and somewhat heavy . . . representing plain, masculine kind of people.' On the treatment of drapery he explained that 'Giotto melted all these folds into broad masses of colour . . . the dresses are painted sternly. . . . Lastly, it is especially to be noticed that these works of Giotto, in common with all others of the period, are independent of all the inferior sources of pictorial interest. They never show the slightest attempt at imitative realization: they are simple suggestions of ideas, claiming no regard except for the inherent value of the thoughts.'

Spencer never went to Padua; he saw the Arena Chapel through Ruskin's eyes, aided by the reproductions he collected, chiefly in the form of Gowans and Gray Art Books, price sixpence. Yet there followed a whole series of paintings of the subjects treated by Giotto. *Joachim among the Shepherds,* 1912 (see fig. 6) is based upon Ruskin's account of the appropriate fresco, while *The Visitation* of 1913 and *Zacharias and Elizabeth* of 1914 (fig. 7) were stimulated less directly by the same. Characteristically, they also have local roots, the one in a particularly beautiful garden Spencer saw in Cookham and the other in life drawings he made of the butcher's daughter and his cousin, the milkmaid. But then Ruskin had identified Giotto's greatness in his 'being interested in what was going on around him, by substituting the gestures of living men for conventional attitudes, and portraits of living

14

6. Study for *Joachim among the Shepherds*. 1912. Pen, pencil and wash, 40.6 × 37.1 cm. (16 × 14⅝ in.) London, Tate Gallery 'Then Joachim, in the following night, resolved to separate himself from companionship; to go to the desert places among the mountains, with his flocks, . . . And immediately Joachim rose from his bed, and called about him all his servants and shepherds, and caused to be gathered together all his flocks . . . and went with the shepherds into the hills . . . ' John Ruskin, quoting B.M. Ms. Harl. 3571

7. *Zacharias and Elizabeth*. 1914. Oil on canvas, 152.4 × 152.4 cm. (60 × 60 in.) Collection Mrs Stephen Bone

8. Paul Gauguin (1848–1903): *Christ in the Garden of Olives.* 1889.
Oil on canvas, 72.4 × 91.4 cm. (28½ × 36 in.) West Palm Beach, Florida, Norton Gallery and School of Art

men for conventional faces, and incidents of every-day life for conventional circumstances.'

Other things were going on around Spencer too, and there can be little doubt of his interest. *John Donne Arriving in Heaven* was selected by Clive Bell for the English section of Roger Fry's second Post-Impressionist exhibition, held at the Grafton Gallery from October to December 1912. It is not difficult to see why Bell chose it. It is the one work of Spencer's which shows an awareness of Cubism, with its tendency to abstraction through simplified, planar forms. For him it was an isolated excercise, similar to the ones with which his fellow student Nevinson was to persist until he produced, a few years later, his distinctive version of English Futurism. Not that Tonks approved of these developments, any more than he did of Fry's first controversial promotion, 'Old Masters of the New Movement', held in the same gallery two years earlier. That exhibition had brought to London in large numbers

16

9. *The Apple Gatherers*. 1912–13.
Oil on canvas, 71.1 × 91.4 cm. (28 × 36 in.) London, Tate Gallery

paintings by Cézanne, van Gogh and Gauguin. It would be difficult to over-emphasize its importance for the younger generation of British artists, who, in the ensuing controversy, united in their admiration for the new art. To some extent the exhibition confirmed existing loyalties, especially among those who had first-hand experience of painting in Paris: Augustus John, Matthew Smith and Duncan Grant, besides Fry himself. But they were all slightly older than the Slade students of 1910 for whom Professors Brown, Tonks and Wilson Steer were the guides and mentors. Among the forty or so works by Gauguin shown at the Grafton Gallery was *Christ in the Garden of Olives* (fig. 8). There can be little doubt that it influenced Spencer in his treatment of *The Apple Gatherers* (fig. 9), a Slade sketch subject for which the original drawing is also in the Tate Gallery. Soon after it was finished, the oil was bought by Henry Lamb, six years older than Spencer and already established as a founder

10. Henry Lamb (1833–1960): *Fisherfolk*. About 1912.
Oil on canvas, 80 × 101 cm. (31½ × 39¾ in.) London,
Fine Art Society Ltd

11. Gilbert Spencer (1892–1979): *The Crucifixion*. 1915.
Oil on canvas, 86.4 × 99.1 cm. (34 × 39 in.) London,
Tate Gallery
Like his brother, Gilbert Spencer attempted to translate
the New Testament into contemporary terms. The head
of Christ is that of their father, William Spencer.
'I don't know what it is,' Stanley Spencer is reported as
having said, 'but when Gil paints Pa his pictures seem
to be all right.' In spite of that encouragement, Gilbert
Spencer seems to have recognized his own limitations as
a painter of religious subjects and 'soon abandoned that,
realising that I could get along better in other ways'.
(Foreword to *Stanley Spencer*, Harvill Press, 1962)

member of the Camden Town Group. Lamb
had spent part of 1910–11 in Brittany, where
he steeped himself in the lingering associations
of the place with Gauguin (fig. 10). He too
exhibited in the second Post-Impressionist
exhibition—a portrait of the Bloomsbury
writer and critic, Lytton Strachey.

The triumph of Spencer's career at the Slade
came in 1912, when he was awarded the
Melville Nettleship Prize and the Composition
Prize for his painting of *The Nativity* (fig. 13).
'He has shown signs', wrote Tonks, 'of having
the most original mind of anyone we have had
at the Slade and he combines it with great
powers of draughtsmanship.' It is a remarkable painting, in which the neo-primitivism of
the figures, with their frozen poses and mask-
like faces, once again recalls Gauguin. Even

the composition, divided horizontally near the
foreground by a wicket fence, with a steep
recession on the left towards a high sky-line, is
reminiscent of certain of Gauguin's Breton
paintings of about 1889, *Bonjour Monsieur
Gauguin* and *Little Girl Keeping Pigs*, for instance. The setting of Spencer's *Nativity* is as
certainly Mill Lane, Cookham, as the background of Gauguin's *Le Christ Jaune* is Pont-
Aven with the Colline Sainte-Marguerite. In
the sharpness of definition, however, he con-
firms his earlier affection for the Pre-Raphaelites, while the kneeling Virgin separated by a
spacious foreground from her child recalls a
fifteenth-century model along the lines of
Hugo van der Goes's Portinari altarpiece.

No picture sums up better the young artist's
achievement. When he sat the entrance exam-

18

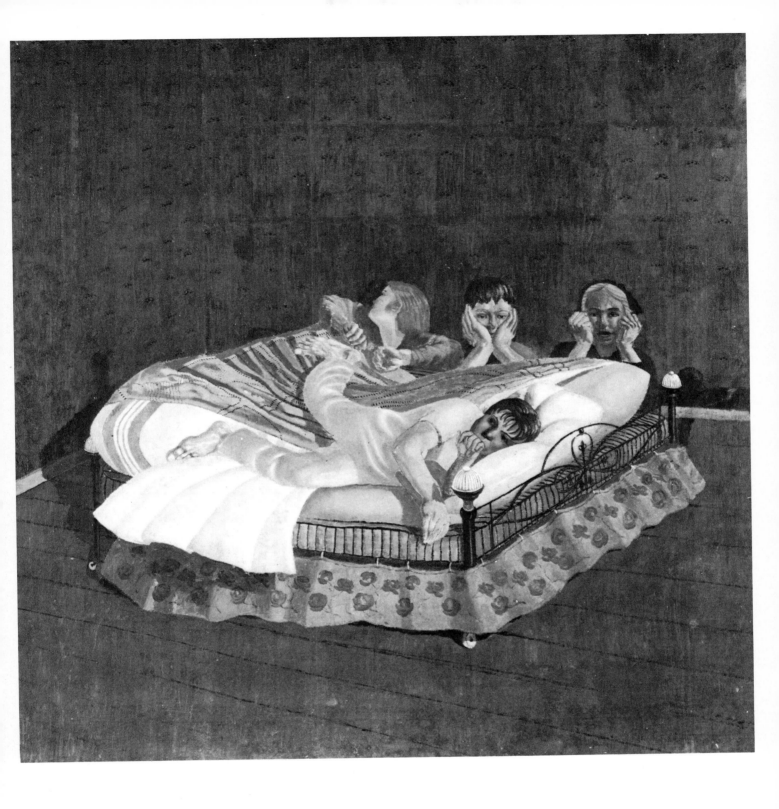

12. *The Centurion's Servant*. 1914–15. Oil on canvas, 114.5 × 114.5 cm. (45 × 45 in.) London, Tate Gallery
Known as 'the bed picture', it depicts the miracle performed by Christ *in absentia*, the healing of the Centurion's servant (Luke 7:1–10). Spencer used the bed in the maid's room at Fernlea, together with members of his family as models, arranged as he remembered his mother describing villagers praying around the bed of a dying man.

ination for the Slade in 1908, he failed the general knowledge paper. By the time he left, he had acquired, in addition to a sound academic training, a familiarity with the most important developments in contemporary art in Europe. He had identified with the 'Neo-Primitives', as those students called themselves who combined a passion for early Italian painting with varying degrees of interest in Roger Fry's *avant-garde* parades. He had also made friends, of a kind he could rely upon to contribute sympathy and ideas through shared interests in a particular kind of painting. Of these, Henry Lamb was to become one of the most unselfishly supporting. After agreeing to buy *The Apple Gatherers*, he released it to Sir Edward Marsh, as important as a patron as he was discriminating as a collector. Shortly afterwards, Lamb bought *The Centurion's Servant* (fig. 12) for himself. At about the same time, he introduced Mr and Mrs J. L. Behrend, two of his own patrons for whom he had painted a portrait (of Mrs Behrend) in 1912. Ten years later they were to provide Spencer with the greatest of all his opportunities.

When Spencer left the Slade, he lived at home and painted either at Fernlea or in one of the several makeshift studios he and his brother Gilbert found in barns and sheds around the village (fig. 11). Far from losing contacts, however, the Spencers attracted a growing number of friends and acquaintances to their Berkshire retreat. Finally, a London taxi brought the ultimate and spectacular compliment, Lady Ottoline Morrell, to the front door of Fernlea. It is not hard to account for the note of pre-lapsarian confidence recollected in Spencer's words, 'When I left the Slade and went back to Cookham I entered a kind of earthly paradise. Everything seemed fresh and to belong to the morning. My ideas were beginning to unfold in fine order when along comes the war and smashes everything.'

13. *The Nativity.* 1912
Oil on panel, 102.9 × 152.4 cm. (40½ × 60 in.) London, Slade School of Fine Art, University College

War

At the end of the war, Spencer returned naturally and inevitably to Cookham. Upstairs in Fernlea he found the canvas of *Swan Upping at Cookham* (fig. 16), which he had left unfinished in 1915. He sat down and completed the painting. In one sense, very little had changed. 'I still felt—more surely if anything—the significance of what I had always felt here.'

He was not demobilized immediately, but was given extended leave to work on *Travoys Arriving with Wounded at a Dressing Station* (fig. 14), the picture commissioned from him by the Ministry of Information. News of the commission reached him while he was still on active service, and a first study for it was lost at the battle-front in 1918. It depicts the transport of wounded soldiers which he witnessed during the Macedonian campaign. In his

22

unfinished autobiography he identified the night when, in September 1916, after the attack of the 22nd Division on Machine Gun Hill in the Doiran-Vardar sector of the battlefield, 'I was at Smol near the little Greek church used this night as an operating theatre. It was a memory of this that I had when I did the *Travoys*.' Spencer painted it in Lambert's Stables, Cookham, where there was a space big enough to accommodate the large canvas.

Soon afterwards, in 1920, he moved a short distance from Fernlea, to the Slessers' house across the river at Bourne End. There he produced, within a relatively short time, a series of religious paintings which are the direct descendants of his pre-war canvases. *Christ Carrying the Cross* (fig. 15) was stimulated by a newspaper report of Queen Victoria's funeral recounted by Spencer's host, Sir Henry Slesser. As one would expect, the scene is set

14(left). *Travoys Arriving with Wounded at a Dressing Station.* 1919. Oil on canvas, 213.4 × 233.6 cm. (84 × 92 in.) London, Imperial War Museum

15(right). *Christ Carrying the Cross,* 1920. Oil on canvas. 152.4 × 142.2 cm. (60 × 56 in.) London, Tate Gallery

17. *Christ's Entry into Jerusalem.* About 1920. Oil on canvas, 114.3 × 144.8 cm. (45 × 57 in.) Leeds, City Art Galleries

in Cookham, on the High Street just outside Fernlea, and includes a couple of local builders' men walking past with their ladders. Characteristically, that explanation, the artist's own, belies the subtlety of their inclusion in the composition. The ladders, apparently

16. *Swan Upping at Cookham.* 1914–15, finished 1919. Oil on canvas, 116.8 × 142.2 cm. (46 × 56 in.) London, Tate Gallery
Men of the Vintners Company annually bring the Thames swans ashore at Cookham to clip their wings.

crossing accidentally, reflect the shape of the true cross. They also add an iconographical reference, with which Spencer would have been familiar from his knowledge of European painting, to the Deposition.

Christ's Entry into Jerusalem (fig. 17) is often dated somewhat later, but in both overall conception and treatment of detail it seems so close to *Christ Carrying the Cross* that it must have been painted around the same time. The best-known of the twenty or so canvases he produced at Bourne End is *The Last Supper* (fig. 19), which hangs now in Cookham Church. It derives from a drawing which Spencer made in 1915; the Upper Room is based upon a local malt-house in which he enjoyed the feeling of seclusion partly induced by the unusual lighting from the low windows. The effect is one of monastic simplicity, reminiscent both of early Italian painting, with the steep foreshortening of the table top and the rhythmic abstractions of the drapery, and of Post-Impressionism. It offers further evidence of the continuity between Spencer's pre- and post-war art. Indeed, in the paintings he produced at the Slessers', he seems to have achieved the kind of concentrated, mystical experience he recalled during the war. In 1917, he wrote a long letter from Salonica for publication in Eric Gill's magazine *The Game*. It is an essay in nostalgia for Cookham, where mystical experience had been part of everyday reality, 'we all go down to Odney Weir for a bathe and a swim. I feel fresh, awake and alive; this is the time for visitations. . . . I swim right in the pathway of sunlight; I go home thinking of the beautiful wholeness of the day. During the morning I am visited and walk about in that visitation. . . . In the afternoon I set out my work and begin the picture. I leave off at dusk feeling delighted with the spiritual work I have done.'

Spencer's use of the present tense is revealing. After two years' absence, under conditions of hardship and suffering, his recollection of Cookham is untarnished and immediate. Inevitably, however, the war also left its own profound impression upon that particularly observant and retentive mind.

The painting of *Travoys* by no means exhausted Spencer's artistic interest in his wartime experiences. These were varied; after initial training he was posted to the Beaufort War Hospital, Bristol, where he found ideas for pictures in the menial tasks he performed as an orderly. In August 1916 he was sent to Macedonia where he served with the 68th, 66th and 143rd Field Ambulances. Then in August 1917 he volunteered and joined the 7th battalion, the Royal Berkshires. In spite of the danger of fighting in the line, he wanted to return to Kalinova, a beauty spot in the mountains for which he yearned. His active service ended shortly before the armistice when physical exhaustion combined with malaria to commit him to hospital in Salonica. 'It would hearten me so if only I could get to do some painting,' he wrote from convalescence to his sister Florence in October 1918. A number of his wartime drawings survive, although others, including the first study for *Travoys*, were lost at the battle-front. Once back in England, Spencer continued to recollect, in drawings and paintings, his thoughts of the war. Two small oil studies on panel, of soldiers in Macedonia making a red cross out of stones and scrubbing their clothes on the rocks of a river-bed, were probably made in 1919. Two years later Spencer was invited by Muirhead Bone, whose efforts had been decisive in obtaining the commission for *Travoys*, to paint a mural for the village hall at Steep. Richard Carline has identified the drawing of *Scrubbing the Floor and Soldiers Washing* (fig. 18) with that scheme. Spencer spent several months with the Bones without further progress, however, and the project was eventually abandoned. A year later he joined his future wife Hilda Carline and her family on an expedition to the Balkans, where they painted side by side in a landscape which reminded him, together with survivals of the Ottoman past, of Macedonia.

Sporadically, his war pictures continued to absorb a part of Spencer's attention. In June 1923 he was staying with his old friend Henry Lamb at Poole in Dorset. Lamb wrote to Richard Carline on 10 June, 'Stanley sits at a table all day evolving acres of Salonica and Bristol war compositions.' By then Spencer

18. *Scrubbing the Floor and Soldiers Washing*. About 1921.
Pencil and grey wash, 25.1 × 36.5 cm. (9⅞ × 14⅜ in.) Cambridge, Fitzwilliam Museum

had already 'drawn a whole architectural scheme of the pictures', to quote from one of his own letters to his future wife, without having any very real prospect of realizing the project. However, among Lamb's visitors that summer were Mr and Mrs Behrend. Spencer reported to Hilda Carline on 19 July that they had greatly admired the designs and soon after 16 September he wrote her the news that they had decided to build a chapel to house the projected paintings, near to their home in the Hampshire village of Burghclere. It was to be a memorial to Mrs Behrend's brother, Lieutenant Henry Willoughby Sandham, R.A.S.C., who had died in 1919 as a result of an illness

he had contracted in Macedonia. Spencer's project, commemorating his own experience of the same campaign, therefore had a relevance to the dead man, although it is clear that the Behrends made no effort to influence the artist's choice of subject-matter. No obvious connection exists between their relative and the hospital scenes in the lower panels, which recall Spencer's service as a medical orderly at the Beaufort War Hospital. As J. L. Behrend freely admitted, 'Without Stanley, poor Hal would have had no memorial.'

At first patrons and painter seem to have toyed with the idea of employing George

Kennedy, an architect with whom they and Henry Lamb were friendly. Basically, however, Spencer had already designed the interior of the chapel for himself (fig. 24). His drawings show that he had not only planned the painted decorations in detail, but had decided upon the proportions of the walls with their divisions by means of arched mouldings into bays. Even such architectural details as the plaster corbels and the shaped dado are clearly indicated. As far as the exterior was concerned, Spencer's preference for simplicity was encouraged by Richard Carline, who argued the analogy with Giotto's Arena Chapel at Padua. No comparison could have been more to the point. According to George Behrend, 'What ho, Giotto!' was Spencer's immediate reaction to the commission. He resolved, presumably on the same grounds, to paint his chapel in fresco, though he was eventually persuaded by technical difficulties to revert to his familiar medium of oils on canvas.

In October 1923, while plans for the chapel were still under discussion, Spencer returned to Hampstead, where he had the use of Henry Lamb's studio on the top floor of the Vale

19. *The Last Supper*. 1920.
Oil on canvas, 91.4 × 121.9 cm. (36 × 48 in.) Cookham, Stanley Spencer Gallery

20. *Resurrection, Cookham.* 1923–6. Oil on canvas, 274.4 × 548.8 cm. (108 × 216 in.) London, Tate Gallery

Hotel in the Vale of Health. He lived, as he had done before, with the Carlines in Downshire Hill. His engagement to Hilda Carline was broken and renewed a number of times before they were married in 1925 at Wangford, near Southwold. Meanwhile, in Lamb's studio, Spencer had begun to work upon a large painting of the *Resurrection* (fig. 20). Sir John Rothenstein described his first visit, 'The room was barely large enough to accommodate the immense canvas, measuring some eighteen feet long by nine feet high, which leaned against the longest wall. Up against the canvas stood a small table—which, with two kitchen chairs and a small tin bath, was the room's only furniture—and upon it a large teapot, half a dozen unwashed plates and some white marmalade jars, some containing paint brushes and others marmalade.' It was a return, for the artist, to the subject he had painted in 1915 and had already envisaged as the culmination of his projected frescoes commemorating the Great War. It was a return also, in spirit, to Cookham. There, in the familiar churchyard, Spencer depicted himself together with a number of his friends, in the company of his forebears on the Day of Judgement. Richard Carline, who recalls posing in the nude for the picture, is readily discernible beside Spencer himself, and Hilda appears several times. It is a deliberately momentous work, in which Spencer seems to be reviewing and revealing all his early debts, both personal and artistic, in the timeless context of his own Thamesside paradise. The Resurrection holds very little terror as it is shown here; indeed Spencer referred invariably to the joys represented. His souls awaken slowly to a reality in which the senses are revived to permit recognition and greeting.

29

They smell the flowers and touch the earth as they adjust to eternal life in Cookham churchyard. There is little hint of damnation, apart from the mild form of scolding which seems to be going on in one or two of the tombs. Instead the atmosphere is one of peace and spiritual ease; it is not inappropriate to find, upper left, Charon transformed into the skipper of a pleasure-boat packed with holiday-makers.

There can be no doubt that Spencer regarded the work as a milestone in his career. It occupied his attention for the greater part of two years and was the focal point of his first one-man show at the Goupil Gallery, in February to March 1927. From there it was purchased by the Duveen Paintings Fund and presented to the Tate Gallery. In the same exhibition a number of war compositions were shown, from the earliest small oil-sketches to more contemporary studies for the Burghclere decorations. Among them were the two drawings for the north and south walls referred to above. By 1927, the Behrends' scheme was well under way. In Lionel Pearson they had found an architect willing and able to design the chapel in accordance with Spencer's wishes. It was dedicated as the Oratory of All Souls by the Bishop of Guildford on 25 March 1927, the feast of the Annunciation—coincidentally or not, the day on which the Arena Chapel was consecrated in Padua, over six centuries earlier in 1305.

In May 1927 Stanley and Hilda Spencer moved, with their baby daughter Shirin, to lodgings in Palmer's Hill Farm, Burghclere.

21(left). Hilda Spencer (1889–1950): *Portrait of Elsie.* 1931. Oil on canvas, 172.7 × 81.3 cm. (68 × 32 in.) London, Anthony d'Offay Gallery
Stanley Spencer's *Country Girl* (1931) is another portrait of Elsie painted against the same background.

22(right). *Hilda and I at Burghclere.* 1955. Oil on canvas, 76.2 × 53.3 cm. (30 × 20 in.) London, Private Collection

23. *Cottages at Burghclere*. 1929.
Oil on canvas, 62.9 × 160 cm. (24¾ × 63 in.) Cambridge, Fitzwilliam Museum

That was a temporary measure until the completion of Chapel View, the house built for them by the Behrends. They were to remain in Berkshire, with interruptions, until 1932. Life there was pleasant. It was recalled nostalgically by Spencer in a number of the scrapbook drawings which he made after 1940 and in the canvases which he based upon them (fig. 22). He and Hilda ran a car and were helped in the house by Elsie, a local girl who became indispensable, especially after the birth of a second daughter, Unity, in 1930. Apart from his work on the chapel, Spencer found time to produce a number of landscapes

(fig. 23) and Hilda continued to paint, influenced by her husband but revealing her own considerable talents (fig. 21).

Before he left Hampstead, Spencer had already painted for the chapel two of the smaller canvases, predellas as he called them, which were destined to occupy the lower sections of the wall. These, together with the larger arch-topped canvases, were stretched in the conventional manner of easel painting and then fastened into the bays. The upper portions of the wall, on the other hand, had to be painted *in situ*. For them, canvas was imported from Belgium to ensure adequately wide

24. Study for the Burghclere Chapel. About 1923.
Pencil and wash, 55.9 × 71.4 cm. (22 × 28⅛ in.) Cookham, Stanley Spencer Gallery

seamless lengths, which could be glued to the wall over an underlay of asbestos cloth.

Once installed in the chapel, Spencer proceeded to paint his way methodically around the walls, beginning with *Convoy Arriving at Hospital with Wounded* (fig. 28) for the bay on the north wall nearest the entrance. It is a typical composition, dominated by the vertical iron railings of the gates, which are shown from that slightly too high viewpoint Spencer enjoyed. The opening of the gates towards the foreground brings the convoy itself, a lorry-load of wounded soldiers, out of the wall and

down, through the foreground towards the spectator. It is a similar compositional device to the one he used in *The Farm Gate* (fig. 65), in which a sense of movement is generated by the diagonals of the opening and by the crowding of the upper surface of the picture, seen in steep perspective. As the presentation drawings make clear, Spencer had already planned each scene in some detail. He introduced only one substantial change; the drawing for the north wall (fig. 24) shows in the third bay an operating theatre in action. In the summer of 1916 Spencer had described to his

34

young friend Desmond Chute his admiration for an operation he witnessed at the Beaufort Hospital. 'It is wonderful how mysterious the hands look, mysteriously intense,' he wrote, and illustrated the point with a drawing in the letter of surgical instruments radiating from the patient's wound. The Burghclere study derives in turn from that, but, for whatever reason, Spencer omitted it from the finished cycle. Instead, the scene of *Kit Inspection* was moved one place to the left and *The Dugout* (fig. 25) was added, as a fourth scene, occupying the bay nearest the altar wall. It is one of the most moving of the Burghclere subjects. Two dugouts are shown in steep perspective at right angles to the foreground. The surface of the deserted earth is brightly lit. Led by the imposing figure of a sergeant in the process of camouflaging his hat, the men emerge on to it from the trenches below in the way that Spencer's souls rise from their graves in Cookham churchyard. Indeed, he described it to Richard Carline as 'a sort of cross between an "Armistice" picture and a "Resurrection"', the fulfilment of a fantasy he had on active service that he and his comrades would awake one morning to find that the war was over. In the chapel, its effect is enhanced by the position it occupies at the east end of the north wall, nearest the altar, a prelude to *The Resurrection of the Soldiers* (fig. 26).

Spencer began work on the altar wall in the autumn of 1928. The focal point of the cycle, both visually and spiritually, it was the composition over which he struggled most. An early study in the Fitzwilliam Museum (fig. 27) differs in a number of respects from the final solution, while a photograph of a working cartoon for the wall in the possession of Richard Carline shows that even at that late stage the foreground was not resolved satisfactorily. Beneath the mules in the centre, fallen soldiers appear, their foreshortened legs sprawling towards the spectator. By contrast,

25. *The Dugout*. 1928. Oil on canvas. National Trust: Burghclere, Sandham Memorial Chapel (Photo: Jeremy Whitaker)
The scene beneath is one of the eight 'predellas' in which Spencer commemorated the routine of life at the Beaufort hospital. In doing so, he concentrated upon those menial tasks which demanded considerable physical effort from the soldiers and orderlies involved. In *Tea-Urns*, the polished metal cylinders challenge the figures in the same way that kit-bags and piles of dirty laundry dominate the adjacent scenes.

27. Study for *The Resurrection of the Soldiers*. c.1927.
Pencil, blue and grey wash, 35.6 × 25.4 cm. (14 × 10 in.)
Cambridge, Fitzwilliam Museum

28. *Convoy Arriving at Hospital with Wounded*. 1927.
Oil on canvas. National Trust: Burghclere, Sandham
Memorial Chapel (Photo: Jeremy Whitaker)

the final solution, with its *trompe-l'oeil* of the lower figures occupying the space behind the altar, is masterly. These almost life-size figures stand on a level with the spectator. They are portrayed as individuals numbed by their common experience, poignant memorials to men with whom Spencer shared a life of hardship, fear and suffering, resulting for so many of them in the death from which he raises them. The simple, identical white crosses of the military cemetery dominate the scene as

26(left). The Sandham Memorial Chapel, Burghclere. 1927–32. Interior view. National Trust

the symbols of their passion. The confused heap of these crosses near the foreground is itself eloquent of the wastage of life, amidst the tangle of warfare. Beyond, towards the figure of Christ in the distance, the crosses become the objects of contemplation for the soldiers who handle them. The message is a transcendental one, of spiritual awareness achieved through sacrifice, of redemption through suffering. Kalinova, the place which made such a deep geographical impression upon Spencer, provided the setting for the Resurrection. Still more of the Macedonian landscape features in the two continuous bands of decoration along the tops of the north and

37

29. *Riverbed at Todorova.* 1930–1. Oil on canvas, glued to the wall.
National Trust: Burghclere, Sandham Memorial Chapel (Photo: Jeremy Whitaker)

south walls. *Soldiers Making a Red Cross* reappears, together with other scenes of encampment and military routine, as a detail of the *Riverbed at Todorova* (fig. 29).

Violence as such is significantly missing from Spencer's recollections of the war. Whether the scenes depict events at the Beaufort Hospital or on the Macedonian Front, they concentrate upon everyday duties. Soldiers are shown cooking and eating, bathing and scrubbing clothes, and picking fruit. In *The Camp at Karasuli* (fig. 30) on the south wall, Spencer painted a portrait of himself as a private picking up litter with a bayonet. Such details reveal his respect for mundane tasks, his ability to 'see Heaven in a grain of sand'. They are a reminder too that he spent the war in the ranks, carrying out his share of such duties close beside his comrades-in-arms. As Wilenski wrote in 1933, 'by the artist's side . . . we smell the flesh of the herded soldiers, we feel the texture of their clothes and towels, the exact consistency of every object they handle'. It has often been pointed out that *Map-Reading* (fig. 32) on the south wall is the only scene directed by an officer. Even so, he is sur-

38

30. *The Camp at Karasuli* (detail). 1930. Oil on canvas, glued to the wall.
National Trust: Burghclere, Sandham Memorial Chapel (Photo: Jeremy Whitaker)

rounded by soldiers at ease, including the group of figures at the top of the canvas who are shown picking berries. The bushes among which they clamber are painted in the sharp focus Spencer delighted to apply to his studies of landscape and vegetation. The colours in this are lighter and clearer than in many of the other scenes, perhaps because he painted it not alongside, but in the house in Cookham to which he and his family moved in December 1931. Elsewhere in the chapel, the dull, earth colours of canvas and khaki predominate.

Spencer's pictorial record of the war is unique. Its simple humanity expressed through the commonplace stands out in contrast against the very different reactions of artists like Nevinson and Wyndham Lewis. They found excitement in the bursting of a shell, in the hot and cold steel of modern warfare. Nevinson's *Study for 'Returning to the Trenches'* (fig. 31) is an exercise in dynamic, uniformed movement, as lacking in sentiment as Wyndham Lewis's design for the cover of *Blast* No. 2 in which men and machines alike conform, in his own words, to 'the hard, the cold, the mechanical and the static'. Spencer could not

31. Christopher Richard Wynne Nevinson (1889–1946): *Study for 'Returning to the Trenches'*. 1914–15. Charcoal and crayon, 14.6 × 20.6 cm. (5¾ × 8⅛ in.) London, Tate Gallery

have been more remote from such abstractions of form and feeling. His observations of his fellow men are warm with sympathy and understanding, like those of the poet David Jones, who mingled the poetry of high romance with everyday speech and earthy wit to describe his own wartime experiences in *In Parenthesis* in 1937. There is an element of catharsis in both; as Spencer explained, 'the Burghclere Memorial . . . redeemed my experience from what it was; namely something alien to me. By this means I recover my lost self.'

The Burghclere Chapel became an object of interest and curiosity long before it was finished. Spencer was visited there by his friends, the Lambs, the Bones and other members of the circle of acquaintance he shared with the Carlines. The director of the Tate Gallery made a point of calling, as did some of the leading lights in Bloomsbury, Duncan Grant and Vanessa Bell among them. By the time the painting was completed the Spencers had moved to Lindworth, a house in Cookham which they had bought in 1931. The return was something of a triumph for the forty-year-old artist. He re-entered the paradise of his youth carrying the laurels of victory and success. His election to associateship of the Royal Academy in 1932 set the final seal of approval upon his achievement.

32. *Map-reading*. 1932. Oil on canvas. National Trust: Burghclere, Sandham Memorial Chapel (Photo: Jeremy Whitaker)

Wilderness

Three years later, Spencer resigned. 'I never wanted to become an associate,' he told a *Standard* reporter, 'I do not approve of the Academy, but I thought the best way to change it was to join it.' He seems to have enjoyed the notoriety he earned by his row with the Establishment. It was caused by the refusal of the hanging committee to include two of the five paintings submitted for the Summer Exhibition of 1935. They found *Workmen in the House* (fig. 34) and *The Builders* (fig. 33) acceptable, along with a landscape, although the building contractor who had commissioned both in the previous year turned them down for being 'not up to specification'. It was not these, however, but the more provocative subjects of *The Dustman* (or *The Lovers*) and *St Francis and the Birds* (figs. 39 and 35) which offended the arbiters of Academic taste.

In spite of the headlines, these incidents serve to illustrate an isolation which was to grow in Spencer's position as an artist. On the one hand he did not belong to the recognized and international *avant-garde* of semi-abstract painters who flourished between the wars; on the other his style did not conform to the standards of realism demanded by popular taste. At Burghclere, his figures had become more rounded and simplified in form, although they did not suffer from the distortions which he introduced later. The rejection of anatomy in favour of simple rounded mass was a tendency in figure painting which Spencer shared with other artists of the period. William Roberts, another product of the Slade School, four years younger than Spencer, abandoned the early influence of Vorticism in about 1928 to pursue an art in which both the subject-matter and treatment reveal more than a slight debt to Fernand Léger. As with Spencer's there is an uncompromising mod-

ernity about his religious painting, and he too encountered opposition. His *Garden of Eden* was rejected by the Carnegie Institute, Pittsburg, in 1929, on the grounds that American taste was not ready for such pictures.

In 1935 the reviewer in the *Daily Mail* wrote, 'Nobody challenges Spencer's ability as a craftsman, the skill of his hand. What many people object to are some of his subjects when these are imaginative conceptions.' He went on to describe *Workmen in the House* as 'a tragi-comedy. A queer-looking carpenter gazes down the length of an enormous saw. Another man is half-way up the kitchen chimney, in the foreground a distracted housewife and her child sprawl on the floor.' In fact the painting represents the kitchen of Chapel View, with Elsie minding Shirin while two workmen mend the fireplace. An equally simple explanation underlies *St Francis and the Birds*. Hilda Spencer provided the key. In a letter she wrote to her husband in 1924 she mentioned that she had been reading in a haystack. As a result, Spencer made a drawing which appeared as one of the illustrations for *August* in the Chatto and Windus *Almanack* of 1927. The figure of St Francis, which is based upon a recollection of his father in a dressing gown, was then 'fitted into the bulk and main lines of what was originally a haystack with a figure reading a book. The back of St Francis takes the line down the front of the figure on the haystack, and the cord round his waist takes the lines of the shoulders and arm of the figure' (*Sunday Graphic and Sunday News*, 28 April 1935). However, the resulting distortion could hardly fail to give offence and it was equally so in the case of *The Dustman*.

33. *The Builders*. 1935. Oil on canvas, 111.8 × 91.8 cm. (44 × 36⅛ in.) New Haven, Connecticut, Yale University Art Gallery, Gift of Stephen C. Clark

42

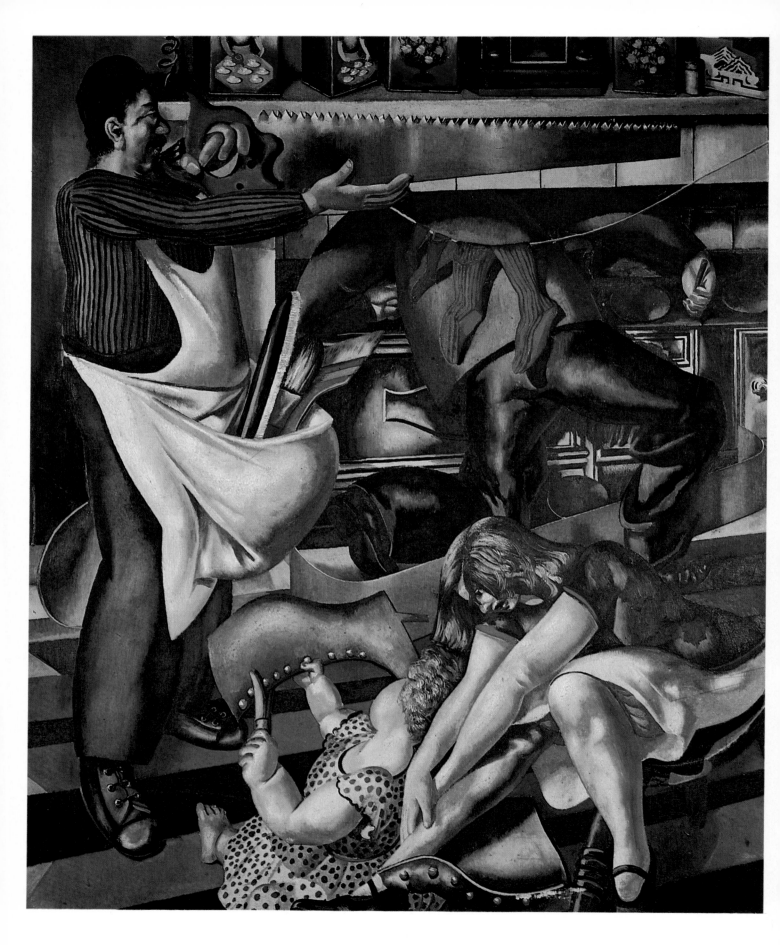

34(left). *Workmen in the House*. 1935. Oil on canvas, 113 × 92.7 cm. (44½ × 36½ in.) Coll. the late W. A. Evill

35(right). *St Francis and the Birds*. 1935. Oil on canvas, 66 × 58.4 cm. (26 × 23 in.) London, Tate Gallery

In the Burghclere Chapel Spencer had glorified the common round of human activity. Thereafter his conviction grew that 'all ordinary acts such as the sewing on of a button are religious things and a part of perfection.' In peacetime no less than in wartime, he relied upon his recollections of everyday experience to furnish the material for his paintings. The very lack of consequence in the events he selected as subjects enhanced their significance and he attached particular importance to rehabilitation: 'I am always taking the stone that was rejected and making it the cornerstone in some painting of mine.' Thus garbage is honoured in the painting of *The Dustman* as an accompaniment to 'the glorifying and magnifying of a dustman. His wife carries him in her arms and experiences the bliss of union which his corduroy trousers quicken.'

In the introduction to the catalogue of his retrospective exhibition at the Tate Gallery in 1955, Spencer explained that 'all the figure pictures done after 1932 were part of some scheme the whole of which scheme when completed would have given the part the meaning I know it had.' He conceived that scheme in these terms: 'the next "chapel" (built also in the air as was the first Burghclere Chapel, that is to say not commissioned) was to be planned somewhat thus: The Village Street of Cookham was to be the Nave and the river which runs behind the street was a side aisle.' Incredible as it may seem, each one of the figure paintings had a place in this chapel in the air, to be filled with scenes of peace and love centred on the village of Cookham. *Sarah Tubb and the Heavenly Visitors* (figs. 37, 38) illustrates one episode from its spiritual history. Sarah Tubb was an old inhabitant of the village, who prayed in the street because she was afraid of Halley's comet. In the painting she is comforted and rewarded by ministering angels, who appear as a matter of course on the scene. In another of the designs for the

Cookham chapel, *Separating Fighting Swans* (fig. 40), the angels bless human intervention from the river bank. Apparently Spencer had attempted that dangerous task himself, some time before 1932. Here the incident may well have been meant to illustrate his role as an artist and more specifically as the architect of the Cookham chapel, with its message of love and concord. However, a subject so closely related to *Leda and the Swan* invites further speculation, especially in view of the other witness, in the foreground, and her pose. It is one of Spencer's earliest references in paint to his *femme fatale*, Patricia Preece (fig. 42).

The Cookham paintings, no less than the project to which they belonged, contained more than a little wish fulfilment. Spencer's return to Cookham coincided with the breakdown of his first marriage. His passionate courtship of Patricia Preece lasted from 1932 until 1937 when they were married, only to separate in the course of a disastrous honeymoon in St Ives. He had hoped to maintain an active relationship with his two wives; an arrangement which neither of them would tolerate, as a result of which he found himself rejected by both. In spite of this practical failure, or perhaps because of it, Spencer became all the more convinced of the need for sexual liberation. He saw it as 'the spiritual goal of humanity, for physical desire exists in human nature in order to aid understanding and add to the joy when it is reached.' It is in the light of such remarks that the full significance of paintings like *The Dustman* becomes clear.

Naturally Spencer's views led him to reject a narrow or moralistic view of Christianity. He singled out St Paul especially as a butt for

36. *Cows at Cookham.* 1936. Oil on canvas, 76.2 × 50.8 cm. (30 × 20 in.) Oxford, Ashmolean Museum

46

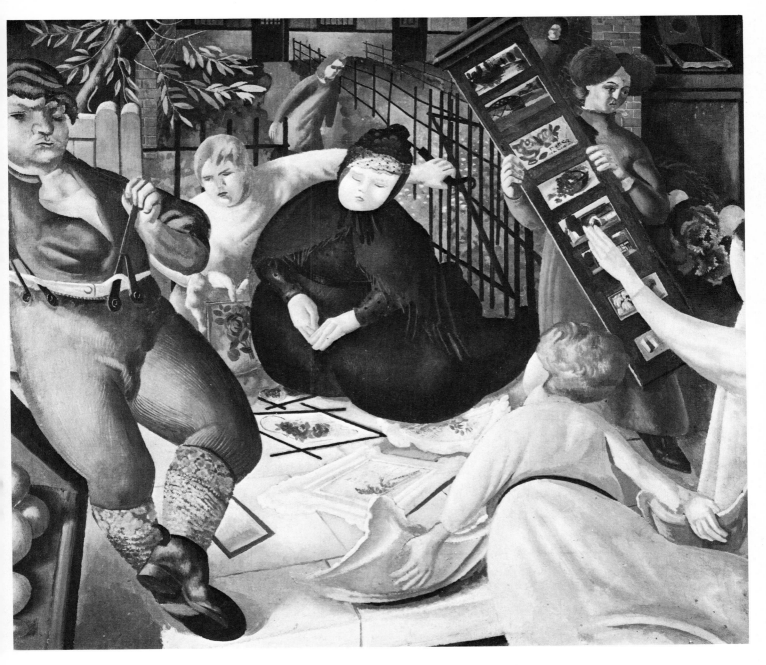

37 and 38. *Sarah Tubb and the Heavenly Visitors*. 1933
Oil on canvas, 94 × 104.1 cm (37 × 41 in.) Private Collection

his dislike of conventional piety: 'He is the originator of all that "get your hair cut" business that caused me so much trouble, he sounds like a Nazi to me.' In his search for a broader and more tolerant view he discovered William Blake, in whose writings he found an anticipation of his own mystical experiences. 'The attractive thing about Blake is that God is found everywhere at all time,' he wrote in 1943. With Blake he began to feel that 'All Religions are One'. He had read Sir Edwin Arnold's *Light of Asia* in Hampstead in the twenties, and recalled in a letter to Hilda: 'I often think of us looking at the books

49

39(left). *The Dustman* (or *The Lovers*). 1934. Oil on canvas, 114.6 × 122.6 cm. (45¼ × 48¼ in.) Newcastle upon Tyne, Laing Art Gallery

40(right). *Separating Fighting Swans*. 1932–3. Oil on canvas, 91.4 × 72.4 cm. (36 × 28½ in.) Leeds, City Art Galleries

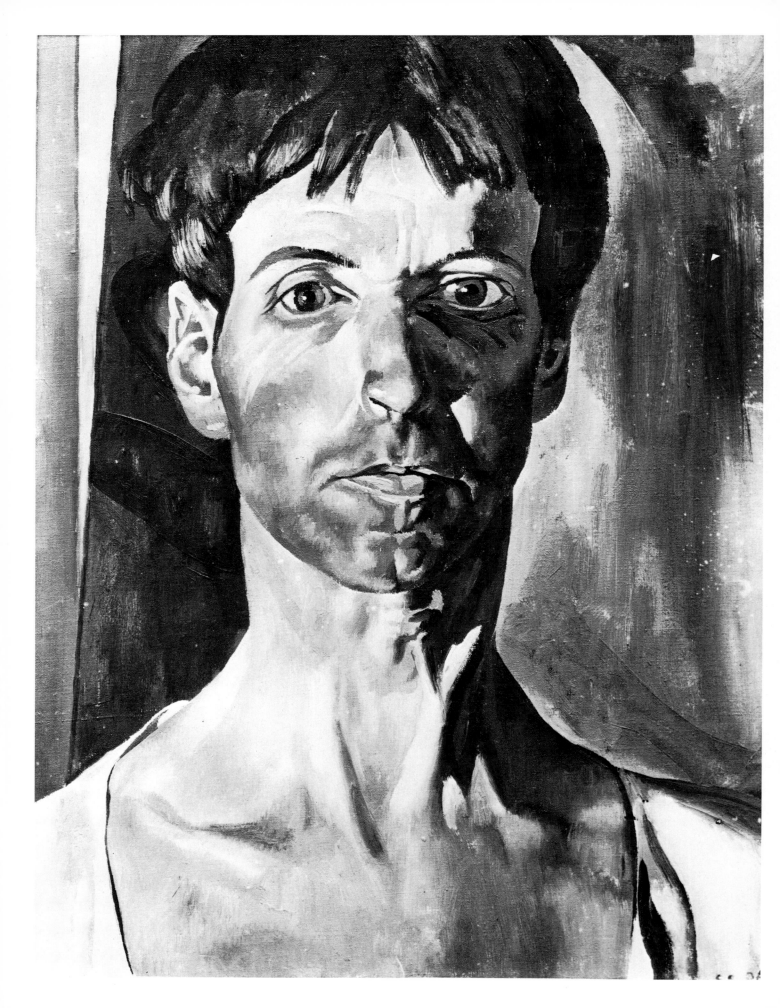

on Indian sculpture. They seem to give me longings greater than those inspired by the Bible.' As his early work shows, Spencer shared the susceptibility of his generation to the influence of non-European art. His confirmed awareness of it is shown, albeit superficially, in a drawing of about 1934 entitled *Mother and Child*. It is a caricature of himself and Hilda as primitive sculptures. At a deeper level he was stirred by the importance of eroticism in oriental art, in which his belief that 'desire is the essence of all that is holy', appeared to be manifest.

Among Spencer's contemporaries there were a number of sexual evangelists. The sculptor and illustrator Eric Gill was inspired by oriental art to invest his religious subjects with frank sexuality. D. H. Lawrence, by means of his novels, preached regeneration of the spirit through the flesh, and primitive cultures served him on more than one occasion as exempla of his theme. In *Women in Love*, for instance, published in 1921, one of the characters defiantly justifies a Pacific carving of a woman in labour as 'Pure culture in sensation, culture in the physical conciousness, really ultimate *physical* consciousness, mindless, utterly sensual.' To this context Spencer's *Love Among the Nations* (fig. 47) belongs. He explained how 'during the war, when I contemplated the horror of my life and the lives of those with me, I felt that the only way to end the ghastly experience would be if everyone suddenly decided to indulge in every degree and form of sexual love, carnal love, bestiality, anything you like to call it. These are the joyful inheritances of mankind.' Emancipated from convention, he felt free to explore, in the paintings of the 1930s, subjects like *Sunflower and Dog Worship*, based upon the cult of Asparsas and

appealing to Spencer because 'the mystery of love is that it can find its abode in something not meant for itself, and yet when it does so, it is clearly its home.'

During the winter 1936–7, Spencer began a series of nudes for which he and Patricia served as the models. The subject of these, the most personal of all his sexual paintings, is their relationship, committed in all its physical intimacy to canvas (fig. 43). The close range and sharp focus were essential; he explained that painting them he liked to feel that he was crawling over the contours like an ant. The *Double Nude Portrait*, also known as '*The Leg of Mutton*' (fig. 49), is still more physically explicit, with the inclusion of a joint of raw meat as a kind of carnal still-life amidst the expanses of gleaming human flesh. Such paintings remained as private as their subject-matter. Spencer's income was derived instead from landscapes. He tended to dimiss these as pot-boilers, out of which he was forced to make a living. Yet the best of them compare favourably with the landscapes of the Nash brothers, his former contemporaries at the Slade. *Cookham Moor* (fig. 46), for instance, is represented with a sensitivity to the tones and textures of atmosphere and distance. It is difficult to see how the painter can have begrudged such delicate naturalism, any more than he resented the lively detail of *Gardens in the Pound* (fig. 48). Indeed both recall his admission that 'the kind of heaven I enter when I do begin to paint I find not at all insipid.'

Meanwhile, Spencer's preoccupation with the Cookham chapel continued. He defined it more closely in a paper dated 1937, from which Collis quotes at length. 'A church and a house combined would perfectly fit the mixture,' he explained, envisaging a site on which a church would be flanked by two private houses and a series of small chapels, each eight feet square. They would contain the various cycles of paintings he had designed to establish

41. *Self-portrait, 1936*. Oil on canvas, 61.3 × 46 cm. (24⅛ × 18⅛ in.) Amsterdam, Stedelijk Museum

42. *Portrait of Patricia Preece*. 1933. Oil on canvas, 83.8 × 73.7 cm. (33 × 29 in.) Southampton, Art Gall. and Mus. Patricia Preece, born 1900, was a student at the Slade and a pupil of André L'hote in Paris. Spencer met her in a teashop in Cookham in 1929; at that time she was sharing Moor Thatch, a cottage near to the War Memorial on the edge of Cookham Moor, with her friend Dorothy Hepworth

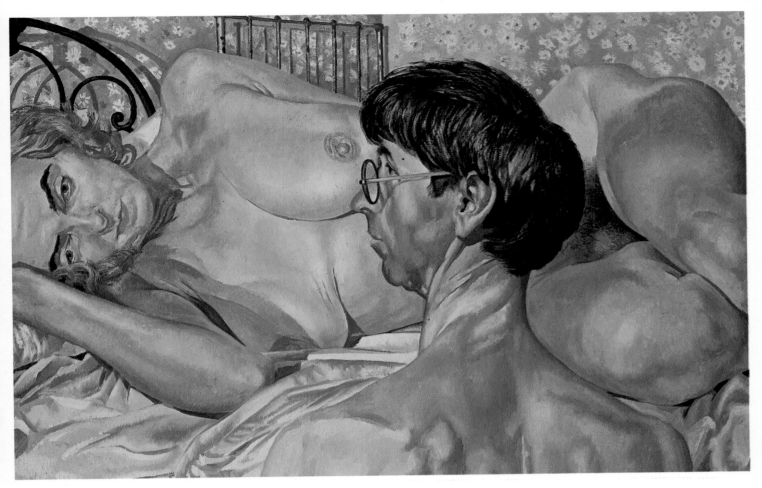

43. *Self-portrait with Patricia*. 1936–7. Oil on canvas, 61 × 91.4 cm. (24 × 36 in.) Cambridge, Fitzwilliam Museum

Cookham as the new Eden of sacred and profane love. From 1936 onwards he produced a series of compositions involving two figures only, man and woman. The earlier of these treated everyday scenes of domestic life, many of them recalled from the early years of his marriage to Hilda; *Dusting Shelves, Taking off a Collar* and the *Chest of Drawers* (fig. 50), for instance. In this last, the sexual implications are clear; the sprawling dominance of the woman is a favourite comment. In turn these pictures were followed by a series of couples called by Spencer the *Beatitudes of Love.* In them the figures are isolated from the kind of background detail he normally provided. They were deliberately distorted to express his notion that in their love they partook of one another physically. 'She is going to give herself to him so that parts of her flesh become parts of his flesh every day,' he wrote of the woman exemplifying *Passion* (fig. 44). About *Contemplation* (fig. 45) he wrote, 'They fit on to or against each other as if they were two parts or two organs of one body. They seem

44. *Beatitudes of Love IV: Passion or Desire*. 1937. Oil on canvas, 76.2 × 50.8 cm. (30 × 20 in.) Collection Lord Walston (photo: David Rowan)

56

45. *Beatitudes of Love V: Contemplation.* 1937. Oil on canvas, 91.4 × 61 cm. (36 × 24 in.) Cookham, Stanley Spencer Gallery

46(left). *Cookham Moor*. 1937. Oil on canvas, 49.5 × 75.6 cm. (19½ × 29¾ in.) Manchester, City of Manchester Art Galleries

47(below). *Love among the Nations*. 193–56. Oil on canvas, 95.6 × 280 cm. (37⅝ × 110¼ in.) Cambridge, Fitzwilliam Museum. The seated figure in a crumpled tweed jacket, his arms around a couple of young negresses, is Spencer himself

48(right). *Gardens in the Pound, Cookham*. 1936. Oil on canvas, 91.4 × 76.2 cm. (36 × 30 in.) Leeds, City Art Galleries

49. *Double Nude Portrait: the Artist and his Second Wife.* 1936.
Oil on canvas, 83.8 × 93.7 cm. (33 × 36⅞ in.) London, Tate Gallery

to find their place of rest where they can best serve each other in the same way as a liver will adapt itself to the shape of a stomach and so on.' Spencer took his Beatitude Couples, like all his creations, extremely seriously. He must have been disappointed by the lack of public sympathy for what he regarded as being of such importance, but even he could not resist the anecdote of Sir Edward Marsh's visit to Tooth's Gallery to inspect them. 'It fogged his monocle; he had to keep wiping it and having another go. "Oh Stanley, are people really like that?" I said "What's the matter with them? They're all right, aren't they?" "Terrible, terrible, Stanley". Poor Eddie.'

At no other point in his career was Spencer so isolated. The estrangement from both his wives left him personally so, and his painting was inaccessible even to some of the staunchest of his supporters. From those lonely frontiers paintings like *Hilda, Unity and Dolls* (fig. 53) are something of a retreat. It is a measure of the Carlines' tolerance and affection that he stayed with them in Hampstead in August 1937; the painting commemorates that visit. However, such efforts, like the landscapes he continued to produce (fig. 54), were interludes. In 1939 Spencer admitted his emotional and spiritual crisis in a remarkable series of paintings of Christ in the Wilderness, remark-

50. *Chest of Drawers*. 1936. Oil on canvas, 50.8 × 66 cm. (20 × 26 in.) Private Collection

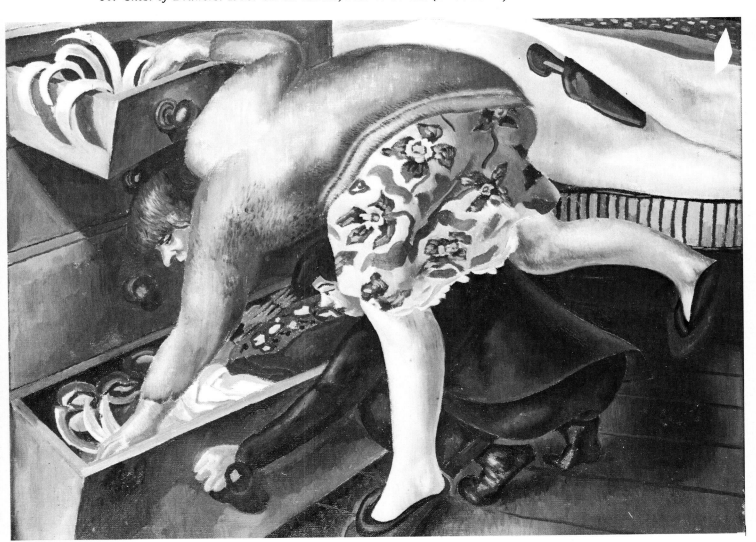

51. *Christ in the Wilderness III: The Scorpion.* 1939. Oil on canvas, 60 × 60 cm. (22 × 22 in.) Collection Helen Brook

52. *Christ in the Wilderness IV: 'Consider the Lilies . . .'* 1939. Oil on canvas, 60 × 60 cm. (22 × 22 in.) Collection Helen Brook

53(opposite). *Hilda, Unity and Dolls.* 1937. Oil on canvas, 76.2 × 50.8 cm. (30 × 20 in.) Leeds, City Art Galleries.

54. *Landscape in Wales*. 1938. Oil on canvas, 55.9 × 70.8 cm. (22 × 27⅞ in.) Cambridge, Fitzwilliam Museum

ably painted. He was living in deliberate isolation in a small flat in Adelaide Road, London. It was there that he conceived the series and painted the first four canvases of Christ alone in the desert, communing with nature (figs. 51 and 52). Each is a remarkable study in introspection, as autobiographical as any of Spencer's paintings. Through detachment from the world, from his emotional tangles and chaotic business affairs, he reached that state of spiritual tranquillity to which mystics aspire. 'Christ is in the Wilderness and the Wilderness Himself,' he explained in a paradox worthy of St John of the Cross. More characteristically, 'I loved it all because it was all God and me, all the time.'

Port Glasgow

Whereas Spencer's war designs had, by the happy chance of enlightened patronage, materialized at Burghclere, the prospects for his Cookham church-house were never more than slight. What he produced for it he regarded, in the retrospect of the introduction he wrote for his exhibition in 1955, as 'excerpts. . . . But as and when I painted them I never felt the joy I would have experienced doing this work had I known that I could complete the scheme.' From this disappointment, and from the wilderness to which the frustrated prophet had exiled himself, he was rescued by the most practical of demands— an important, public commission.

Soon after the outbreak of the Second World War, Dudley Tooth had written to Sir Kenneth Clark, chairman of the War Artists' Advisory Committee, to suggest that Spencer should be employed as an official war artist. As a result he was interviewed in March 1940 and at once proposed a vast Crucifixion with a predella comprising scenes of the current war. The official reaction was a cautious one; instead it was agreed that Spencer should visit Lithgow's Shipyard in Port Glasgow to

55. Study for *Shipbuilding on the Clyde*. Signed and dated: 'Stanley Spencer, May 1940'.
Pencil, 34.3 × 48.3 cm. (13½ × 19 in.) London, Imperial War Museum

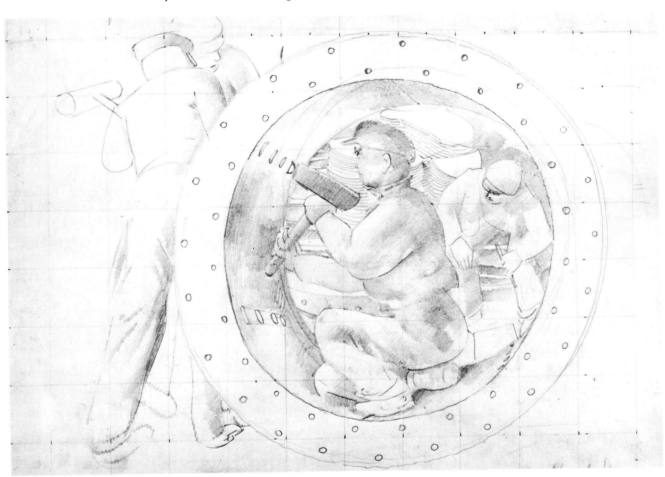

56. *Shipbuilding on the Clyde: Burners*. 1940. Oil on canvas. Triptych, centre section 106.7 × 152.4 cm. (42 × 60 in.) sides each 50.8 × 203.2 cm. (20 × 80 in.) London, Imperial War Museum

consider the possibilities of painting the war effort there. His initial visit was a great success, resulting in innumerable sketches (fig. 55) and plans for an ambitious series of shipbuilding pictures.

In Port Glasgow, Spencer rediscovered his natural sympathy for humanity; not in the abstract, but in the concrete form of a cohesive work-force of real people. Like Cookham, the shipyards had a strong sense of community. Like his regiment in Macedonia, the men performed their varied duties and practised their several skills together, orchestrated invisibly by the purpose and the orders they shared. Off-duty, they revealed their more human side as they sat on a propeller, for

57. *Shipbuilding on the Clyde: Riveters*. 1941.
Oil on canvas, 76.2 × 579.2 cm. (30 × 228 in.) London, Imperial War Museum

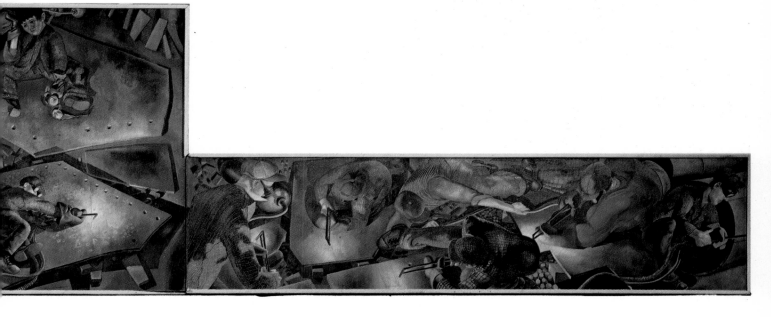

instance, eating sandwiches. Such minor details were characteristic of Spencer's observations and found their way inevitably into his designs. Above all, he responded to the visual stimulus of his unusual subject-matter. He set to work almost at once and the first section of the series, the triptych *Burners* (fig. 56), was completed by the autumn of 1940. In it he accentuated the peculiar conditions, the improbable angles, the strange equipment, and the startling and unnatural lighting effects he saw in the yards. As a result he managed to convey something of

his, the outsider's awe of Vulcan's forge, with all its mysteries. 'I was as disinclined to disturb them,' he wrote, 'as I would be to disturb a service in a church.'

Burners was an instant success. In response to it, the War Artists' Advisory Committee encouraged Spencer's ambitions to extend his shipbuilding series into a loosely constructed polyptych some 73 feet long. His visits to Port Glasgow continued, therefore, and three more sections, including *Riveters* (fig. 57), were completed in 1941–2. He stayed for a month or so at a time, in a guest-

58. *The Resurrection: Reunion.* 1945. Oil on canvas. Triptych, centre and sides each 76.2 × 50.8 cm. (30 × 20 in.) Aberdeen, Art Gallery

59. *The Resurrection: Port Glasgow.* 1947–50. Oil on canvas, 214.6 × 665.6 cm. (84½ × 262 in.) London, Tate Gallery

house near the docks, where he seems to have enjoyed his anonymity among the shipyard people. 'I like it here,' he wrote to Hilda, 'being lost in the jungle of human beings, a rabbit in a vast rabbit warren.'

Some months before he became an official war artist, Spencer's thoughts had begun to turn again to the theme of Resurrection. Then, 'one evening in Port Glasgow, when unable to write due to a jazz band playing in the drawing-room just below me, I walked up along the road past the gas works to where I saw a cemetery on a gently rising slope. . . . I seemed then to see that it rose in the midst of a great plain and that all in the plain were resurrecting and moving towards it. . . . I knew then that the Resurrection would be directed from this hill.' Gradually his documentary interest in the shipyards waned in favour of a visionary one. As he got to know and to love them Port Glasgow and its inhabitants became worthy, in Spencer's eyes, of his redemption (fig. 59).

At first, he planned a single canvas, larger than any he had painted hitherto. This was then resolved into a series, the painting of which occupied him for five years, between 1945 and 1950. In *The Resurrection: Reunion* (fig. 58) he explained, 'I have tried to suggest the circumstances of the Resurrection through a harmony between the quick and the dead, between the visitors to a cemetery and the dead now rising from it. These visitors are in the central panel, and the resurrected are in the panels right and left.' Among the neat rows of sepulchral wrought iron, intentionally reminiscent of the geranium-filled terrace gardens he loved to paint, Spencer included himself and his two wives. 'Here I had the feeling', he wrote, 'that each grave forms a part of a person's home just as their front gardens do, so that a row of graves and a row of cottage gardens have much the same meaning for me. Also although the people are

69

60. *The Resurrection with the Raising of Jairus's Daughter.* 1947. Oil on canvas. Triptych, centre section 76.8 × 88.3 cm. (30¼ × 34¾ in.), sides each 78.1 × 51.4 cm. (30¾ × 20¼ in.) Southampton, Art Gallery and Museums

adult or any age, I think of them in cribs or prams or mangers. "Grown-ups in prams" would express what I was after.'

The side-panels of *The Resurrection with the Raising of Jairus's Daughter* (fig. 60), completed in 1947, were drawn in 1940 before Spencer's first trip to Port Glasgow. He was then living with his friends George and Daphne Charlton at the White Hart Inn, Leonard Stanley, Gloucestershire. The

central window-scene, however, was a Port Glasgow invention and the triptych joined the others; by 1950 he had painted five triptychs and three single canvases. Had a way been found of keeping them together, the ensemble would have rivalled the Burghclere Chapel in size and importance. No such solution was found, and the Port Glasgow *Resurrections* can be seen side by side only in book form; in 1951 *Stanley Spencer: Resurrection Pictures*

was published with extensive notes by the artist and an introduction by R. H. Wilenski.

Like Spencer's other apocalyptic visions, these are homely affairs, devoid of reproach or punishment. The charity of his Last Judgement is everywhere apparent, not least in the painting of the *Angels of the Apocalypse* (Private Collection). It stems from his desire to paint skies filled with angels to go above *The Resurrection: The Hill of Sion* (Preston, Harris Museum and Art Gallery), in accordance with the first verse of chapter sixteen of the Book of Revelation. However, he transformed the seven angels commanded to 'pour out the vials of the wrath of God on to the earth' into divinely appointed ministers of agriculture; they distribute seed and fertilizer instead. It is easy to smile at the homely domesticity of the vision, but that is to deny the seriousness and consistency of Spencer's faith. Convinced as he was of the unity of creation, 'the wholeness of things' as he put it, he could neither discard nor condemn any particle of his own intensely human experience.

Last Years

In the years following the Second World War, Spencer's renown as an artist rose to new heights. He remained, all the same, a controversial figure. Sir John Rothenstein has described the rough passage of *The Resurrection: Port Glasgow* (fig. 59), the last of that series to be completed, into the Tate Gallery in 1950. As he wrote in 1956, what worried him most was the hostility of 'the artists whose work I most admired and whose opinions I generally respected'. Indeed, to them, Spencer's art may well have appeared to be twenty years out of date. In his style there was no significant change after 1930 to 1935, the period in which the simplified figures of the Burghclere Chapel evolved towards the expressive distortions of *St Francis* and the *Beatitudes of Love*. When compared with slightly younger artists whose development had continued over a longer period of time, he must have seemed distinctly *passé*. It was a fate he shared with William Roberts and Edward Burra in a period when the thirties were out of fashion and younger artists interested in the figure looked up to Henry Moore as the prime mover of a new abstraction. At a more popular level, however, Spencer was identified with the *avant-garde*. Remarks like Sir Winston Churchill's famous rebuke, 'If that is the Resurrection, then give me eternal sleep,' merely enhanced the reputation with that whiff of notoriety which Spencer never shunned. On the contrary, the public discovered, in Gilbert

61. *Cookham from Englefield.* 1948. Oil on canvas, 76.2 × 50.8 cm. (30 × 20 in.) Executors of the late G. G. Shiel (on loan to Stanley Spencer Gallery, Cookham)
Englefield was the house of the late Gerard Shiel, who commissioned from Spencer five paintings of his house and grounds. This was the first.

Spencer's words, 'that as well as being a painter, he was a personality.'

Fame did not deprive Spencer of the unassuming manner which was as much the key to his personal success as it was to Charlie Chaplin's. Popular admiration for the more accessible of his paintings was compounded by affection for the more endearing side of his eccentricities. Photographers recorded his familiar course down Cookham High Street, as he set out of a morning shabbily dressed and pushing all the paraphernalia of his painting in a cart made from an old perambulator towards some chosen spot. It was an image of himself he cherished, 'Yesterday I was on my pitch in the Churchyard at 7–10 and it was very cold,' he wrote to Dame Mary Cartwright on 3 August 1958 (fig. 62). The demand for the landscapes which he produced during and after such expeditions continued to rise. Like the figure pictures, they are painted in the style he formed thirty years earlier, perhaps slightly more thinly painted in drier colours, but at their best, achieving similarly impressive results (fig. 61).

Day-to-day correspondence also shows that Spencer was a busy man. Sittings, like other appointments, had to be fitted into the tight schedule of a public figure who found himself called upon to speak in support of various causes. In 1954, he went as a member of a cultural delegation to China. Honourable reinstatement to the Royal Academy came in 1950. The retrospective exhibition held at the Tate Gallery five years later seemed no more than his due. Finally, in 1958, he was knighted.

'The paintings I do now', Spencer wrote in the introduction to the 1955 exhibition, 'are "selected" from hundreds of drawings which I have had by me for many years.' It is true of pictures like *The Farm Gate* (fig. 65), presented to the Royal Academy as his Diploma Painting in 1950, and *The Dustbin, Cookham,*

73

62. *Mary Lucy Cartwright, DBE*. 1958. Oil on canvas, 76.2 × 49.5 cm. (30 × 19½ in.) Cambridge, Girton College

Dame Mary Cartwright was Mistress of Girton College, Cambridge (1949–68). Her sister had been a pupil at the Ruskin School at Oxford where Gilbert Spencer taught.

purchased by the Academy in 1956. Both are straightforward, 'public' works, derived from much earlier drawings. The same connection with the past obtains in the case of a further group of paintings, which had a far greater personal significance for the artist. *Love Letters* of 1950 (fig. 63) has already been cited; a sketch for it appears in a letter to Hilda dated 22 May 1930. *Hilda and I at Burghclere* (fig. 22) is one more example of Spencer's use of a fifteen-year-old drawing to re-create with paint on canvas an episode from the life he shared with his first wife twenty-five years before.

These last may serve to show how Spencer's powers of 'selection' operated at a deeper level. During the years of mental and physical illness which preceded Hilda Spencer's death in 1950, he never accepted the reality of their separation. He maintained one-sided the interminable correspondence which had begun with their courtship and which ended after more than thirty years not with her death, but with his own, nine years later. In these 'love letters' and in his paintings alike, Spencer combined reminiscence of an idealized past with plans for the future. *The Marriage at Cana: Bride and Bridegroom* (fig. 64), painted in 1953, returns to one of the themes for the church-house conceived in the thirties. The principal figures are Hilda and Stanley Spencer in a painting which refers back to their actual marriage and forward to their second marriage envisaged by the artist. Spencer proposed that improbable reunion first in 1942. He returned to the subject frequently during the remainder of Hilda's life and dwelt even more fervently upon it in the years following her death.

Between 1949 and 1954 he painted *Love on the Moor* (fig. 67) as a tribute to her. In the painting she is celebrated as Venus, goddess of love, a devotional image placed on Cookham Moor. She appears eternally young and voluptuous in an especially Spencerian

74

63. *Love Letters*. 1950. Oil on canvas, 86.4 × 116.8 cm. (34 × 46 in.) Collection Professor and Mrs N. B. B. Symons

way. The abased figure crouched at her feet and reaching upwards towards her thighs represents both Spencer and Everyman; the relationship between the figures is an impersonal variant of his characterization of *Me and Hilda, Downshire Hill* (fig. 66). Behind the statue, deliberately painted with the same full curves and fleshy roundness, lies to the right the head and shoulders of a contented, spotted cow. To the left, the same pattern of the cow's hide becomes that of a woman's dress, its wearer occupied in another Hilda-associated activity—reading letters. The rest of the moor is peopled by couples who greet one another and make love in honour of the deity. The atmosphere is a cross between one of Spencer's Resurrections and a Village Fair by Bruegel. The inhabitants of

64. *The Marriage at Cana: Bride and Bridegroom.* 1953.
Oil on canvas, 66 × 50.8 cm. (26 × 20 in.) Swansea,
Glynn Vivian Art Gallery and Museum
In the same year, Spencer painted another canvas
entitled *Marriage at Cana* (Private Collection), and drew
in sepia a composition related in theme, *Servant
Announcing the Miracle* (Private Collection)

65. *The Farm Gate.* 1950. Oil on canvas, 88.9 × 57.2 cm.
(35 × 22½ in.) London, Royal Academy of Arts.

the canvas are lovable in themselves, or
'bloody wonderful' as Spencer would have
described them, enlivened by all their different
human imperfections and treated with the
gentle ridicule he reserved for his *comédies
humaines.* They give and receive presents,
smell flowers and try on clothes, all familiar
pastimes with a special signficance in Spencer's

art. The rites take place at the centre of his
personal universe. Cookham Moor is represented on the canvas with a freshness of
observation which betrays his unfailing devotion, manifest in such details as the irregular
shape of the boundary wall and the tufty
lushness of the meadow grass. No other
finished picture sums up so completely

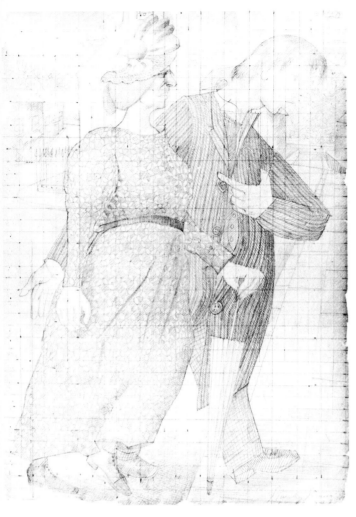

66. *Me and Hilda, Downshire Hill.* After 1944. Pencil, 40.6 × 27.9 cm. (16 × 11 in.) Astor Collection of Scrapbook Drawings.
An unfinished canvas squared up from this drawing was exhibited by Anthony d'Offay, 27 September - 28 October 1978

Spencer's final achievement. It also heralds the two vast canvases, each over 120 square feet, which were to occupy the last years of his life.

Even if Spencer's word for it did not survive, the late works would prove the continuity of his vision and purpose. In spite of the inevitable dispersal of his pictures by sale, he preserved an almost Platonic notion of his life's work to which the church-house would have given tangible form. During the last decade of his life he planned to make two further ambitious additions to it, both as important to him personally and artistically as the *Resurrection* of 1926. *The Apotheosis of Hilda* was designed as a testament to all his sexual loves with one supreme, the one he could attain only by means of his art. In its final form that wish remained, perhaps inevitably, unfulfilled.

A similar fate awaited his other major undertaking. In one of the letters written to Hilda soon after her death, he outlined his plans for a series of paintings of *Christ Preaching at Cookham Regatta.* Though not conceived of as part of the original church-house, they clearly lent themselves to it, and when Spencer drew out his designs, some sixty of them in red chalk, in 1952–3, he allotted to them a river-aisle. In bringing Christ in person back to Cookham, Spencer was returning to his preoccupation of before and after the First World War, when he had set so many scenes from the New Testament in and around the village. For the *Regatta*, he delved still further backwards into memories of his early childhood. As Gilbert Spencer recalled, 'the regattas we knew were Edwardian . . . [they] always emphasized class distinctions; there were those on the river and those on the bank. Those on the river collected themselves in groups, according to rank, and floated about together holding on to one another's boats and punts, looking like gay little floating islands.' *Listening from Punts* (fig. 69), one of the few finished sections of the project, may well have coloured his reminiscence; in any case, it is a vivid, pictorial counterpart both of the era and of the event.

The central section of the *Regatta* was to occupy a canvas more than seventeen feet long. By 1955, Spencer had squared it up and

67. *Love on the Moor*. 1949–54. Oil on canvas, 79.1 × 310 cm. (31⅛ × 122⅛ in.) Cambridge, Fitzwilliam Museum

68. *Christ Preaching at Cookham Regatta*. 1959.
Pencil and oils on canvas, 207 × 534 cm. (81½ × 211 in.) On loan to the Stanley Spencer Gallery, Cookham

69. *Christ Preaching at Cookham Regatta: Listening from Punts.* 1954.
Oil on canvas, 96.5 × 144.8 cm. (38 × 57 in.) Collection Mrs Bronwen Astor

drawn it out in his usual way (fig. 68). The old horse-ferry barge moored by the Ferry Hotel was to provide Christ with a pulpit, and, to guarantee the high viewpoint he favoured, Spencer chose Cookham Bridge as the stand from which he could review the whole village on parade. Characteristically, the sermon is his own. It demands not wrapt attention from the audience, but enjoyment of the experience. They are not celestial bodies but ordinary examples of common humanity, cheerfully inhabiting their earthly paradise, for which the only other word is Cookham.

70. *Self-portrait, 1959.* Oil on canvas, 50.8 × 40.6 cm. (20 × 16 in.) Private Collection

80